Career Quest

EXPLORING FASHION DESIGN CAREERS

KELLEY BARTH

TWENTY-FIRST CENTURY BOOKS / MINNEAPOLIS

Twenty-First Century Books™
An imprint of Lerner Publishing Group, Inc.
241 First Avenue North
Minneapolis, MN 55401 USA

For reading levels and more information, look up this title at www.lernerbooks.com.

Main body text set in Bembo Std Regular.
Typeface provided by Monotype Typography.

Library of Congress Cataloging-in-Publication Data

Names: Barth, Kelley author
Title: Exploring fashion design careers / Kelley Barth.
Description: Minneapolis : Twenty-First Century Books, [2026] | Series: Career quest | Includes bibliographical references and index. | Audience: Ages 11–18 | Audience: Grades 7–9 | Summary: "Fashion design is a booming industry worldwide. From dreaming up a design to handing it off to a customer, learn about this creative field and how to kickstart your career in it"—Provided by publisher.
Identifiers: LCCN 2025011258 (print) | LCCN 2025011259 (ebook) | ISBN 9798765662700 library binding | ISBN 9798348029555 paperback | ISBN 9798765699980 epub
Subjects: LCSH: Fashion design—Vocational guidance—Juvenile literature
Classification: LCC TT507.5 .B37 2026 (print) | LCC TT507.5 (ebook) | DDC 746.9/2023—dc23/eng/20250716

LC record available at https://lccn.loc.gov/2025011258
LC ebook record available at https://lccn.loc.gov/2025011259

Manufactured in the United States of America
1 – CG – 12/15/25

CONTENTS

INTRODUCTION

Take a moment to think about the clothes you are wearing. What fabrics are they made of? Perhaps they are made from cotton, denim, polyester, or even silk. Are the fabrics solid colors, or do they have patterns such as stripes or plaid? How do the clothes fit? Are they loose and flowing or tight and clinging? What type of embellishments are included on each item? Are there buttons, zippers, clasps, or pockets?

Every detail you see on your clothing, down to the color of the thread, was a specific choice someone made. Careers in fashion and design are more than just making a red-carpet outfit for a celebrity appearance. Fashion design impacts all our daily lives. It also influences the trends and styles that often define moments in history.

Careers in fashion design allow people to bring their creativity to an always changing and influential line of work. This book will explore different career paths in fashion design. You will learn about these different career paths and explore ways to pursue these careers both now and in your future.

A person window shops, keeping an eye out for new fashions at a retail store.

CHAPTER ONE

Design Is All Around Us

Many people only think of big, brand-name designers when they hear the word *fashion*. Names including Calvin Klein, Ralph Lauren, Louis Vuitton, and Coco Chanel have become synonymous with fashion. You could probably name many more brand-name designers and fashion companies.

But these high-end brands aren't the only names in the big business of fashion. After all, everyone needs clothing. And behind all clothing, whether it is on the runways of Paris or at the bottom of your laundry hamper, are groups of passionate people working in careers of fashion and design.

Art Meets Business

The fashion industry is one of the largest industries in the world. It is also a huge source of jobs in the United States. Designing, making, and selling clothing and accessories is a multi-billion-dollar business.

Runway shows help designers establish more business and sell their creations.

Careers in fashion design are often a good fit for creative and artistic individuals. Successful designers understand the aesthetics of a garment. They need to have a keen eye for color, pattern, and style. Understanding the artistry of fashion is a useful start.

But designers also need to have strong business sense. They need to understand what consumers want in their fashion. Successful designers also need to create new fashion trends instead of just following them. Most designers play an important role in marketing and selling the garments and items that they design. Fashion is a perfect career choice for someone who loves the mixture of art and business.

The Design Process

The process of designing and making clothing and accessories can look different depending on the individual designer and the company or brand they work for. But for the most part, the process of designing often includes the following stages: research, sketching, prototyping, and manufacturing. Designers follow these general stages and principles to ensure that the garments they create help make fashion that is marketable to consumers.

Research

It is important for designers to be aware of current fashion trends. Reading fashion publications, going to fashion shows, and participating in fashion industry trade groups can help designers stay relevant in their field. One well-known industry group is the Council of Fashion Designers of America (CFDA). The CFDA shares resources and information about fashion design with its members.

Staying up-to-date on fashion trends is critical for designers who are creating new clothing. If a designer creates a clothing line that is dated and no longer considered fashionable, they will have a hard time selling their clothing to people. An important part of a career in design is making sure you are creating products that will be popular and desired.

But fashion designers don't just follow trends. They create them. Following trend research helps designers predict what styles and trends might become popular next. Research is often the key to deciding what styles a designer should create. It is an important first step in inspiring the ideas behind the

Sketches help translate a designer's artistic vision for a garment.

eventual designs. Research also allows designers to know more about their consumer base and the fashions and styles people are interested in.

Sketching

After designers have done their research and have an idea in mind, they often start sketching their concept. Sketches help take an idea and put it on paper. They are an important tool in being able to visually share ideas with other people in the design process. Designers often go through multiple rounds

Finding Creative Inspiration

Careers in fashion design require creative thinking. Designers often need to think outside the box in order to create new styles and garments that haven't been seen before. But constantly coming up with new ideas can be challenging. Here are some tips to help you tap into your own creative thinking:

Start with Action

Some people shy away from design careers because they worry that they aren't creative enough. But creativity doesn't just happen out of nowhere. If you wait for a light bulb moment of inspiration to come to you, then you might be waiting a very long time. The good news is that you don't need to wait for a moment of inspiration. You can be creative and start the process of design even without inspiration. In fact, starting with action and taking charge of your own creative process can be just the thing to inspire you! Grab a piece of paper and start doodling without a goal of what it might become. Maybe as you continue, it will turn into a new design. Maybe it won't. Either way, it is a great way to warm up your creative thinking.

Turn to New Sources of Inspiration

New ideas usually don't come out of nowhere. Designers often turn to other fields to inspire and influence fashion ideas. Look at the shapes, colors, and patterns that can be found in nature. Think about how you could use those styles in your own design. Try researching different time periods throughout history. How can you take old styles and trends and make them new and fashionable? Tap into your interests to create new ideas. Whether you like sports, music, comics, or even animals, your interests can be a powerful driver for creativity.

Develop Your Creative Routine

Where do you do your best thinking? Do you think best in a quiet environment? Or perhaps you prefer listening to music. Are you most energized in the morning or at night? Take some time to design your own environment. When you are in a space that makes you feel creative, it is easier to be creative.

Believe in Yourself

Remind yourself that you are a creative person, and you have interesting ideas to share with the world. If you hit a roadblock on your path to creativity, take a short break. Go for a walk outside, do a puzzle, or draw something just for fun with no pressure about what the result will look like. Don't give up on your creativity. Whenever you feel stuck, try something new!

of sketches as their idea becomes clearer and more developed. Initial sketches may be simple, quick drafts of a general idea. Once the designer has a solid foundation for their idea, further sketches can explore details of the garment such as color, fabric, or embellishments.

Prototyping

Once a sketched design is finalized, it is time to take the idea off the page and make it three-dimensional. Designers make a sample of the product called a prototype. This sample gives them a better idea of what the final product will look like and what changes may need to be made to the design. Designers can then try their prototype on a model and see how it fits and moves on a real person.

Prototyping allows design teams to collaborate and problem-solve if there are any issues with the initial design. Early prototypes are often made from cheaper materials, so they are not as expensive to produce as a final product. This is beneficial because designers may go through multiple rounds of prototypes before they finalize the physical design.

Manufacturing

Once a final design has been decided on, and the designer has a successful prototype, the design needs to be manufactured into a real garment. Manufacturing can take different forms. Some very high-end boutique designers may hand sew a custom outfit with just one person in mind. This is also common in costume design—for example, when the designer only needs one unique costume for a specific actor in a role. Custom manufacturing can be very expensive as it is time-consuming.

Sewing and garment construction skills help designers prototype their styles.

More often, designers need to find a way to manufacture many versions of a garment and sell that garment online or in stores. In mass manufacturing, designers also need to think about how the garment can be manufactured in multiple sizes to be able to fit different body types.

CHAPTER TWO

The Business of Design

There are several different careers in the field of fashion design. Each career has its own specific focus. Investigating different career options is a great way to start thinking about what path may be the best fit for your own interests and skills.

Some fashion designers specialize in one specific area. Other people enjoy the challenge of designing for a wide variety of consumer needs. All designers must work with different types of budgets, materials, and goals.

The average fashion designer makes approximately $79,000 a year. Fashion designers just starting out in their career can expect to make at least $37,000 annually. At the higher end, the top 10 percent of earners make over $160,000 a year. Salaries often range depending on what areas of fashion someone focuses on. If a designer owns their own fashion line, their pay will also depend on how popular their designs are.

Fashion is a collaborative business. It often takes many people working in different roles to make a garment.

Clothing Designer

Clothing designers are also sometimes called fashion designers or apparel designers. There are many different types of clothes that a designer can specialize in. Some designers focus on bridal gowns or formalwear outfits that would fit in at a red-carpet event. Other designers specialize in everyday casual apparel such

Just like clothing designers, accessory designers sketch out their ideas when creating new jewelry.

as T-shirts, jeans, or hoodies. Some designers focus on activewear that people wear to play sports, outerwear including coats or jackets, or even swimwear.

Some fashion designers also design their own textiles, or fabrics. Other designers focus solely on creating the fabrics and materials that other designers use. These textile designers need to have a broad understanding of different types of fabrics and how they work. They often need a good eye for color and pattern and should understand how to dye fabric.

Whatever type of apparel a designer focuses on, they need to understand the types of fabric that are used. Designers need to take into account how each fabric moves and fits. Stretchy spandex works much differently than stiff denim, and strong designs should reflect that difference.

All clothing designers also need to have a solid understanding of who their client is. They also need to think about where the person would go in the garment. Is this a garment that someone would wear to school or to the beach? Consumers have different clothing needs depending on the time of year, location, and even time of day. It is important for all designers to understand what story they are trying to tell with their designs and who their audience is.

Accessory Designer

Designing isn't just for clothing. Many fashion designers focus on other accessories such as purses, belts, or hats.

Footwear designers, for example, create new styles of shoes and boots. They need to pay special attention to how a shoe functions in addition to how it looks. High heels and sneakers have very different functions, but they both need to be able to support the weight of an entire person walking in them all day long.

Jewelry designers create rings, bracelets, watches, earrings, and more. They need to be comfortable working with non-fabric materials such as metal, wood, or gemstones. But accessories aren't only for people. Some designers can also focus on creating plush toys or even pet fashions.

Unlike most fashion designers, not all accessory designers need to know how to sew. Metalsmithing, woodworking, leatherwork, knitting, and sculpting are all skills that could be helpful for accessory designers depending on their area of expertise. Accessory designers also need to have a vision for how their accessory can enhance an outfit.

Costume designers often work with nontraditional materials to help bring characters to life.

Costume Designer

Costume designers typically work on movie or television sets. They can also design costumes for live events such as plays or musical performances. Costume designers work within a set budget to help make the look of a show or performance come together in a way that fits a director's vision.

Costume designers often need to tap into their creative problem-solving. One day, they may be sewing a monster costume from scratch, and the next day, they may be designing an outfit that would work for a performer walking on stilts. They often have to do a lot of research and have a strong knowledge of fashion throughout history. When designing outfits for a different time period, costume designers need to think about what types of fabrics and clothing were available and popular at the time.

Costume designers working in movies and television make an average of $99,000 a year. This field of design is very competitive. Only about 3 percent of all fashion designers work in the movie and television industry.

Additional Careers in Fashion

Designing isn't the only career option available to people interested in fashion. Designers work alongside teams of people who all help bring clothing and accessories to your closet. If you have a passion for fashion but don't love the hands-on aspect of sketching and sewing, some of these careers might be the right choice for you.

Who Designers Work With

Designers also rely on additional people to play important roles in the fashion industry. These fashion professionals help manufacture garments and market new styles to the public.

Patternmakers

Patternmakers play an important role in helping bring fashion designs to clothing racks and closets across the world. Patternmakers create patterns or blueprints that help manufacturers produce large amounts of clothing based on the original designs. They need to have a love of fashion and strong math skills to help mark and cut fabrics to fit different body sizes. The average patternmaker makes around $67,000 a year.

Models

Models help bring fashion to life. Designers can sketch beautiful clothing on paper, but putting a creation on a model helps others to see what those clothes look like on a real person. Sometimes an idea works well on paper or in theory but not as well on a body. Models demonstrate how a design actually functions. They allow designers to see how people move around in their clothing. Models often work in print and digital ads or walk the runway at fashion shows.

The average model makes around $47,000 a year. There are no specific educational or training requirements for models. Designers and retailers are starting to change the way they see models. Many clothing lines are embracing more diversity in their models. There are more opportunities than ever before for models of all races, genders, body types, and abilities. Even so, modeling is an incredibly competitive field that often has a short career span and sees little to no employment growth.

Fashion Stylists

Fashion stylists play a key role in helping certain clothing and looks become popular. They can work one-on-one with celebrities to help dress them for special events. Stylists also work with designers to help accessorize models and put together successful looks for a photo shoot or runway show.

Fashion stylists typically make between $23,000 and $38,000 a year. There are no specific educational or training requirements for fashion stylists. However, having a degree or internship experience in a fashion field can help. It is most important to have a portfolio with styles and looks that demonstrate your ability.

Buyers

Fashion buyers order and purchase garments from designer teams in order to make the items available for sale directly to consumers. Buyers often work for retail spaces such as department stores. They choose what garments and items will be sold in those stores. Buyers should have a strong understanding of fashion, business, and style trends. The average fashion buyer makes around $77,000 a year.

Merchandisers

Merchandisers also typically work in retail stores that sell apparel and accessories directly to the public. They are in charge of the look and design of the retail space. Merchandisers design window displays and choose how to present the clothing and accessories to make them look appealing to shoppers. People in this career should have a strong artistic vision and an understanding of consumer wants and needs. The average fashion merchandiser makes approximately $62,000. This is a very competitive field with few positions available.

Fashion Marketers

Fashion marketers work to advertise designs and products to consumers. They help craft advertising campaigns to create awareness and excitement for the products. Marketers need to have a good grasp of the needs and wants of consumers who are likely to purchase that fashion brand. There is a wide range of pay in the field of fashion marketing that depends on how long individuals have been in their careers and what brand they are overseeing the marketing for. Salaries often range between $64,000 and $239,000.

Strong spatial awareness and a keen eye for color are helpful skills for fashion merchandisers.

CHAPTER THREE

A Day in the Life of a Designer

Depending on a person's specific job, there is typically a lot of variety in a designer's day-to-day work. The different steps in the design process help make every day unique. Some days, designers may rely on their creative brains while they spend their time researching or thinking about new design concepts. Other days, they may engage in more technical, hands-on skills such as sketching or sewing a potential design. If you are someone who likes having variety in their day-to-day work, then a career in fashion may be a good fit for you.

When choosing a career, it is important to look at the work environment and schedule and think about if that career could fit in with your desired lifestyle. Let's dig a little deeper into what life is like as a fashion designer.

Where Is the Fashion Industry?

Much of the fashion industry is concentrated in large, urban cities. In the United States, New York City and Los

Milan's busy fashion district attracts customers from all over the world.

Angeles are the largest centers of fashion industry jobs. Internationally, Paris, France; London, England; and Milan, Italy, also have well known fashion industries with a variety of career opportunities.

However, you do not have to live in one of those cities to have a career in fashion. There are opportunities for a fashion career in almost every large city in the United States. If you are self-employed, you can even live in a more rural area while designing your clothing collection.

If you do live and work in a smaller fashion market,

your work may allow you to travel, especially during large industry events, such as New York Fashion Week. Designers often travel multiple times a year to attend fashion shows and other industry events. Sometimes they also travel abroad to meet with manufacturing teams or material suppliers. Travel can even be a great source of inspiration for many designers.

Large workshop spaces with good natural lighting help designers work through all of their design steps.

Work Environment

Fashion designers primarily work indoors. Many may work mainly in an office setting. But most designers also have larger workshop spaces. Designers need space to cut, sew, and work hands-on with fabrics and materials to bring their designs to life.

Wholesale Company Designers

Most fashion designers work for wholesale companies or manufacturers. These companies sell clothing and accessories to retail or online stores. Those stores then sell the designs directly to consumers. Being employed by a wholesale company can give designers the opportunity to design in multiple different areas and practice different skill sets. Designers may have the opportunity to design T-shirts that are sold at a Target store and Halloween costumes for dogs at the same time. Many designers enjoy this variety in their work.

The wholesale work environment also often has more stable working hours and schedules. While extra work may be required to meet deadlines at certain times of the year, typically wholesale designers do not have to work many weekends or evenings. Wholesale designers also tend to work with a bigger team in which everyone plays a specific role in the design process. Working for a wholesale design company also allows designers to have the support and resources of a larger company behind them, which often means better working benefits and a steady paycheck.

Q & A with Fashion Designer Ann Emerson Reem

How did you decide on a career in fashion design?

I was always drawn to apparel and fashion. When I was younger, I would go to the grocery store with my mom, and I would beg her to buy me fashion or bridal magazines because I loved seeing all the pretty dresses. Occasionally she would buy me one, and I would read it cover to cover, tear out pictures, and draw on them until the whole thing fell apart!

How did you first start designing?

I've been sketching my whole life. When I was five, my mom started buying me sketchbooks, and I would just fill them all up with fashion sketches. I was also completely obsessed with Barbies, so I started sewing clothes for my Barbies. They weren't very good at first, but it was just so fun to make them! I would use any spare fabric that I could find, even taking old socks that my family would throw away and cut them and stitch them into Barbie dresses. It was my creative outlet. My grandma was a seamstress and taught me to sew at a young age. I would go to her house every Sunday, and we would sew for hours.

What steps did you take to pursue your career in fashion design?

In high school, I started learning more art forms, like drawing, painting, and ceramics, and I took a lot of sewing classes as well. This helped me begin to learn the technical aspects of sewing construction. I eventually found a fashion design program and graduated with a BS [bachelor of science] in fashion and retail with an emphasis in design and development. I learned everything from sewing to technical sketching to CAD [computer-aided design], and eventually designed a clothing line and presented at a fashion show. I had two internships in college and took on as much freelance work as possible. All of this helped me secure a full-time fashion design job after college.

What is your favorite part of your job?

My favorite parts are using my core design skills, like sketching, sewing, and illustration. Fashion illustration is so fun because I get to make things look awesome and really bring concepts to life. I love working with colors and material selection as well. It's so fun to see and touch all these beautiful garments and be a part of what will come out next season. I also love that I can use the creative and the technical sides of my brain, so I never get bored and do something new at work every day.

What advice would you give to someone interested in this career path?

If you are interested in fashion in any way, I'd say go for it! There is a place for you in the fashion industry no matter what your skill set is. No matter if you have ten years of experience or zero years of experience, there is a place in the industry for you, and if you have that passion, you will do an amazing job and you will thrive. Go do what you want to do and don't be scared.

A large crowd gathered for the Marc Jacobs runway show at New York Fashion Week in 2019.

Self-Employed Designers

Another employment option that appeals to many fashion designers is self-employment. Approximately 9 percent of fashion designers are self-employed. Some self-employed designers might do freelance, or short-term project work, for larger companies. But often, self-employed designers have their own fashion brand where they create high-end, custom garments.

There are a number of pros and cons of being self-employed. These designers get to choose their own hours and work schedules. They have complete creative control over what projects they choose to take on and the designs they make. This can create a sense of pride and freedom for many people. However, being self-employed also comes with challenges. When you are self-employed, you are in charge of every aspect of your company. If your clothing line doesn't sell, then you don't get paid. It can be a high-risk but high-reward situation.

Work Schedule

Most fashion design jobs are fast-paced. There can be occasional pressure to perform at a high level under strict deadlines. If you are considering a career in design, it may be good to think about what type of pace you work best in. Do you like taking your time to sit with an idea for a while? Or do you prefer an environment with hustle and bustle?

Fashion designers also have a lot of variety in their work depending on the time of year. Many fashion lines release large seasonal collections in the spring and fall. Other brands choose to release new styles on a rolling basis every month. Work deadlines may be especially strict if a seasonal collection needs to be finished soon. Production deadlines or fashion shows are often important dates that designers are working toward. Self-employed and freelance designers especially may need to work long hours on evenings and weekends to make sure their designs are finalized on time.

Work Challenges

No job is without its challenges, and fashion design is no different. Design can be a very competitive career path. There are many talented and creative designers who compete for a limited number of positions. New designers starting out in the field may need to be extra flexible in where they choose to work as they gain more experience and build their portfolios. Starting your own fashion line and brand is particularly competitive. While it is a dream for many people, very few fashion designers will ever have a brand that becomes a household name.

Fashion design is also often a high-pressure career. Many designers feel the need to always keep designing new and successful styles. Designers need to always be on the cutting edge of fashion. If they create designs that don't sell and aren't popular with consumers, their job or fashion line may be in trouble. As Heidi Klum, the host of the fashion design reality television show *Project Runway*, often said, "In fashion, one day you're in and the next day you're out."

Choosing just the right fabric to work with can make the difference between a successful garment and a flop.

CHAPTER FOUR

How to Pursue Your Design Dreams

Now that you have a better idea about what a career in fashion design could look like, it's time to investigate how to follow this career pathway. There are some important qualities and skill sets that serve fashion designers well.

Designer Personal Qualities

Above all, fashion designers bring a love of fashion and a sense of creativity to their work. These are two of the most important qualities to possess when pursuing a career in fashion. Even if you aren't planning to go into the design field and are more interested in being a buyer, merchandiser, or marketer, creativity and a love for fashion are essential. But there are other important personal qualities that are also important for people in the fashion industry.

Interpersonal Skills

Interpersonal skills help you work with others. No matter

Learning to sew and create patterns are essential skills for fashion designers.

what type of fashion career you have, it is very likely that you will have to get along with and work well with others. Design can often be collaborative. Especially when you work for larger companies, teams share ideas and work together to produce the best product. Designers need to be strong communicators. They have to share their vision and designs with other designers, marketing professionals, models, and consumers. Designers also need to be open to receiving feedback about their designs. Constructive feedback can be both positive and negative. Designers who share and receive constructive feedback are more likely to become better designers over time.

Business Skills

Fashion designers need to understand and keep up with the business side of fashion. They need to be able to produce high-quality garments under strict deadlines. Designers often manage multiple projects at the same time, so time management and multitasking are important skills to have. Many designers also have to make sure that they are paying attention to budget when designing their products. They need to understand how much money it will cost to produce a garment and how much money that same garment could be sold for in a retail setting. Strong designers are also detail oriented. Paying attention to even small elements of a garment, such as what color thread is used, can make the difference in the success of an item. Finally, designers are problem-solvers. They are flexible and can adapt to situations. Problem-solving is another opportunity to practice out-of-the-box creative thinking, so it is an area where many designers excel.

Building Your Technical Design Skills

Many careers require interpersonal and business skills. But fashion designers also need to have several technical skills that are specific to their designing process. The good news is that you don't have to wait until college or your career to start building your technical skills. In fact, it's possible that some of your interests and hobbies may already be the basis for some of this important knowledge. And if you haven't started on these skill sets yet, don't worry. Now is a great time to get started!

Sketching

Sketching is a very important skill that fashion designers use frequently. Almost every design starts from a simple sketch. Practice sketching all different types of bodies and clothing. As you continue, start refining your sketches. Choose one design you are excited about and sketch it from different angles. Try playing with scale in your sketches so you can focus on smaller details. As you become a more capable sketcher, try adding color, patterns, and other details to your designs.

There is no right or wrong way to practice sketching. Many designers prefer to start on paper and then eventually move on to a tablet or computer. But others start directly on a screen. Try both styles and figure out what works best for you.

Sewing

Sewing is perhaps the most important skill for a fashion designer to have. Learning how to sew, both by hand and especially with a sewing machine, is essential to a career in design. In the past, many family members passed down sewing skills to new generations. But if you don't have anyone in your life to teach you how to use a sewing machine, don't despair. There are still many options for people who are passionate about learning. See if your school has coursework that teaches basic sewing skills. If not, look into other community courses that may be offered near you. Ask around at fabric and craft retail stores to see if they offer introductory classes. Reach out to family and friends to see if anyone has an old sewing machine sitting around collecting dust that you can experiment with. There are also plenty of

Basic sewing skills give aspiring clothing designers an avenue for making their designs come to life.

free sewing tutorials online. These resources can be helpful for both beginners and more advanced sewers who are looking to learn a new skill.

Using a sewing machine can feel daunting at first, but don't give up. The persistence it takes to learn how to sew will be a huge help in your future, as designers need that same level of persistence. As you learn to sew, it is also a good time to start learning about different fabrics and materials. Different materials function in different ways, and a well-rounded designer needs to know how to work with them.

Sculptural Arts

Spending time doing other types of art can also be helpful to many designers. This is especially true if you are more interested in designing footwear, accessories, or jewelry. Any type of 3D sculpture art practice can be very helpful for people interested in these design fields. But even if fabric is your passion, taking courses in sculpture, woodworking, metalsmithing, or ceramics can benefit your designs as you learn how to work with those materials. Being comfortable with a wide variety of materials and artistic skills is often helpful as you create new designs.

Coursework to Prepare You for the Design Field

If you are passionate about a future in fashion design, you don't have to wait until college to start preparing. Almost every high school offers plenty of courses that will come in handy as you build your design skill set. Obviously, any courses that teach sewing or fashion design skills will prepare you for your next step. But don't be afraid to think outside the box. There is a lot that future designers can learn from all sorts of different subjects.

Art

Introductory coursework in drawing is a great choice to add to your transcript. Not only can you hone your sketching and drawing skills, but these art courses may also help you build the initial portfolio that will benefit you in your next steps. Depending on your interests, taking coursework in other artistic mediums including digital art, painting, sculpture,

Business courses can teach you the financial and marketing skills to help you run your own fashion line.

ceramics, woodworking, and jewelry making can also be beneficial.

Business

As discussed previously, fashion is often a combination of art and business. Taking business courses such as entrepreneurship or marketing will help prepare you for the business side of a career in fashion. This is especially important if you think you may want to be self-employed and run your own fashion line someday. Courses in personal finance and budgeting will also help you develop business savvy and money management skills you will need in your career.

English, Speech, and Communications

Fashion designers have to be clear communicators in order to share their designs and work with the world. Learning to write persuasive arguments and becoming a comfortable public speaker will assist you in your design career.

History and Social Studies

Designers often turn to history and other cultures outside of their own as inspiration in their designs. Studying history and geography can deepen your understanding of fashion throughout a variety of times and places. Plus, looking for ways different coursework can tie into a deeper understanding of fashion will allow you to keep honing your creative mind.

Math

Fashion couldn't exist without math. Designers need to make sure that their measurements are precise. Having a solid math foundation will also help you manage budgets and scale designs for production. A strong basis in geometry is particularly helpful.

Science

Even though most people think of fashion as an art, that doesn't mean there isn't still science involved. In fact, many fashion design programs have lab opportunities to learn more about the science behind different fabrics. Students often put clothing through experiments during which they see how different fabrics hold up under intense heat, light, friction, and even fire.

Technology

Most designers frequently use computers to enhance their design process and help with logistics. In particular, coursework in CAD programming or 3D printing could be helpful. You'll learn more about the role of technology in design in chapter five.

How to Choose a College for Your Design Career

Choosing the right college can often feel overwhelming. With all the options and information out there, how do you begin to choose the right pathway? While there are thousands of colleges in the United States alone, fewer than a hundred offer

a bachelor's degree in fashion design. If you are certain that fashion is the field for you, then the best way to start narrowing down your college options is to look for a school that has a major in fashion design or apparel design.

One great place to start your college search is with College Navigator, a website run by the National Center for Education Statistics. College Navigator has a helpful search function so you can find college options based on what majors they offer.

Using your major to narrow down a potential list of colleges is a good starting point. But there is more to think about. Where in the country do you want to live? Would you prefer a large, busy university or a smaller, more personal college? Research the personality of the college and its students. If possible, visit the college in person to see if it feels like a good fit for you.

Another important element to look at when choosing a college is the outcomes for students. As mentioned previously, fashion is a competitive career field. It is important to choose a college that will help set you up for success in your career. Don't be afraid to contact college admissions offices and ask questions about their fashion design programs. Some questions you may want to consider include: What percentage of new graduates go on to find jobs in the fashion world? What types of jobs do new graduates typically find? What type of career service help does the college offer? Does the college help students find internship opportunities?

If you want to learn more about studying fashion design and college in general, the website Big Future is a great place to start. Big Future offers a variety of resources to help you research careers and plan for college.

College and Beyond

Most fashion designers have a bachelor's degree, which is needed for the majority of careers in the industry. But some designers are self-taught and did not go to college. After all, if you are self-employed, there are no strict educational requirements. However, this pathway is less common and can be more challenging if you are hoping to work for a company. Most employers prefer to see a college degree in design.

Internships and Apprenticeships

Many college students studying fashion participate in an internship or apprenticeship with a design company. At some colleges, participating in these hands-on industry experiences is a mandatory part of the coursework needed to graduate. But even if a school doesn't require it, getting some real-world experience is often helpful for your future career.

Building a Design Portfolio

One of the most important tools in your fashion career is your design portfolio. A design portfolio helps showcase your talent, ability, and style. A strong design portfolio is important to demonstrate your design strengths and styles to potential employers or clients. Your portfolio needs to tell a story about who you are as a designer and what you want to say to the world through your creations. Even with a college degree and coursework, employers want to see your design style and skills for themselves.

Design portfolios are also important when applying to college. Many fashion programs will expect to see a portfolio of your work and designs in your application materials. Do your research and make sure you include the information that each individual college is asking for. In general, you should be prepared to show detailed sketches of multiple design projects, often from different phases of the project. You should also share photos of your completed designs. Portfolios are intended to show your process, not just the final result. It's never too early to start building your portfolio. And remember, it is a living, changing document. Just like your designs, don't forget to adjust and revise your portfolio as you go.

A design portfolio helps share your artistic vision with potential clients and employers.

CHAPTER FIVE

The Future of Design

Fashion design is a slowly growing field. The Occupational Outlook Handbook run by the US Bureau of Labor Statistics predicts that opportunities in fashion design will continue to grow about 5 percent between 2023 and 2033. This is about as fast as the average job market is growing. They predict that every year during that period, there will be approximately 2,100 fashion design job openings. Most of these jobs, however, will be working for larger companies. Opportunities for self-employed designers are likely to become even more competitive. It will likely be more challenging for smaller businesses to compete with larger companies in the future.

While it is slowly growing, fashion is also an always changing field. This is part of what makes these jobs so appealing. An important part of a designer's job is to be on the cutting edge of trends and changes in the field. Trends in fashion include current popular colors, patterns, and cuts. It is easy to see how some clothing has changed over time. Take denim jeans, for example. Whether they are bell bottoms,

CAD programs have advanced the design process, which is especially beneficial for footwear designers.

acid-washed, bootcut, skinny, distressed, or wide-legged, jean trends and styles are constantly changing and adapting. As a designer, it is important to both follow and create style trends.

Larger fundamental trends throughout the twenty-first century also influence how we see fashion. Fashion design has often served as an important reflection of culture and

Sustainable clothing options have become increasingly popular in recent years.

what society's priorities are. As society changes, fashion changes alongside it, and vice versa. Here are a few of the larger social conversations that are happening in the world of fashion.

Sustainability in Design

The fashion industry brings a lot of important artistry to the world. But it also creates a large amount of waste and contributes to pollution. The fashion industry is responsible for 10 percent of global carbon dioxide output and 20 percent of plastic produced each year.

However, consumers have started becoming savvier about how their fashion choices impact Earth. Consumers want to support fashion brands and products that use sustainable practices and materials. They want clothing that makes them look good on the outside and feel good on the inside.

Fashion designers are listening. The consumer demand for sustainable fashion has impacted the way many designers and manufacturers approach the industry. More than ever, designers are embracing vegan, recycled, and other eco-friendly materials. Many brands are also embracing using natural fabric dyes and working on ways to decrease water usage in fabric construction. People want quality and sustainable clothes that will last over time, and much of the design industry is working to make that happen.

Inclusive Design

Just as designers are searching for ways to make fashion more environmentally friendly, they are also working to make clothing more accessible and inclusive to all people. Fashion brands both large and small have started creating clothing lines with a focus on adaptability. They recognize that everybody is different. Not only is there a need for expanded sizing options, but consumers with physical disabilities also need individual pieces that fit and function with their set of needs in mind. This is one way in which designers are reassessing the needs and desires of their clients. Author Jonathan Kaufman explained, "Adaptive fashion opens the doors for a new talent pool to develop skills from the technical sides such as textiles, and design, to marketing and brand development."

Creating garments that work for a variety of body types is a key goal of many fashion brands.

The fashion industry has also been focusing on how to make both garments and the industry itself more welcoming and inclusive. This is an area that many young consumers are passionate about, but there is still a lot of work to be done. Many brands have embraced an increase in diversity regarding race and ethnicity, body size, and disability when it comes to their products and advertising. Models, runway shows, and ad campaigns have steadily become more inclusive over the last few years. However, that inclusion hasn't quite made its way into the staff that fashion brands employ, especially at the highest levels of management.

In order to continue setting trends, increased inclusivity in the workspace is one area that fashion needs to embrace. Inclusive environments are good for business as they often provide a wider variety of options to more customers. Fashion companies that have more women and people of color in charge typically financially outperform companies that are less diverse. A diverse workforce is better able to address the needs of diverse clients. Jamie Gill, founder of the Outsiders Perspective, a nonprofit for people of color in fashion, summarized this, saying, "Having the right people around the table, having those fresh perspectives from all different walks of life is really what we need to look at."

Designers attempt to tell a story with the clothing collections that they create and manufacture. Many designers are trying to incorporate clothes that are sustainable, accessible, and inclusive in their design stories. While there is still more improvement and work that can be done in all areas of diversity and inclusivity, people are having conversations that they weren't having in the past. Hopefully, these conversations will continue to push the field of design forward in new ways.

Changing Technologies in Design

While design trends change over time, so does the technology that helps propel fashion forward. Designers have to be comfortable using computer programs to bring their designs to life. Initial design sketches used to all be done by hand. However, as technology has advanced, fashion designers have begun using CAD programs to help them bring further details to their sketches.

AI and Fashion

Artificial intelligence (AI) is influencing many different careers, and the field of fashion is no exception. In fact, there are many interesting and exciting ways that AI can benefit fashion designers. One major way that AI is impacting the field is through the clothing manufacturing process. AI can make more accurate predictions of future sales and trends than most individuals can. These predictions help companies better manage their inventory and estimate how many items they should produce and order.

However, there are also some downsides and potential concerns about the impact of AI. Some people are worried that AI will take over human jobs. Other experts disagree. They caution that jobs aren't going to be lost to AI, but they will change and evolve. AI is a powerful tool. But at the end of the day, it is just a tool that needs a person to run it. Human designers bring an important understanding to the design process that AI isn't likely to replicate.

Another concern about AI-driven design is that over time, designs will all start to look the same. AI-driven fashion would be less unique and groundbreaking. This shift runs the risk of making fashion less appealing and popular to consumers. AI is excellent at analyzing large amounts of data and making conclusions based on that data. But it isn't able to truly innovate ideas. AI can only create concepts from data that already exists. Human creativity knows no limits, and the AI of today just can't compete. It could also run the risk of creating concepts that are too similar to other designers' original work.

AI is likely here to stay and will continue to impact the ways that people in the fashion industry do their jobs. But don't worry. Fashion career opportunities are continuing to grow, and AI is more likely to remain a helpful tool than replace jobs.

Many designers still start sketching on paper and then take their ideas to the computer. Using CAD technologies, they turn their sketches into fashion illustrations that include more details about the fabric and color. CAD programs also allow designers to better visualize what their designs will look like by placing them on a virtual model. This process allows designers to create more precise measurements and patterns before prototyping their garments. This can help save time and resources as designers can more easily make adjustments before they are working with real fabric.

Many designers are also turning to 3D printing to find new ways to express their creativity. While fully 3D printed outfits are not yet practical and available to retail consumers, this technology does help expand the concept of what is possible. Some high-end designers are experimenting with how 3D printed elements can enhance their runway fashions. Utilizing 3D printing is especially useful in creating fashion accessories such as jewelry or embellishments such as buttons. This technology is also a helpful tool for many brands, especially in footwear design. Companies use 3D printing in their prototyping stage and beyond to push their innovative designs further. The shoe company Adidas, for example, started collecting data about how athletes run. They then utilized that information to 3D print custom shoes to enhance running performance. As technology advances, many in the fashion industry are looking for ways it can benefit the entire design process.

CONCLUSION

Design with Confidence

Creative careers, including fashion design, can be challenging. In order to succeed, you don't only need to have creativity. You need to have confidence. It takes a lot of confidence to share your ideas with other people. It takes even more confidence to send your designs and products out into the world for everyone to judge and scrutinize.

It is important to remember that even the most successful fashion designers in the world don't appeal to every consumer. People have different styles, tastes, and preferences. It takes confidence to tune out the negative voices and keep focusing on your creativity and design. Designers often need a thick skin in the face of criticism. Some people may love your designs. Other people will most certainly not. You cannot control how consumers or critics will perceive and review your designs. But the good news is that you can control your level of confidence in how you approach your work.

The right clothes can make the person wearing them feel confident. It's equally important for fashion designers to have confidence in the clothing that they create.

Confidence doesn't just come out of nowhere. The best way to increase your confidence is to keep working on your design skills. The best fashion designers know that they are never done learning and growing in their field. Practice and experimentation are crucial to growing your design skills. Embrace the idea of always trying something new, especially the things that scare you. Try working with new fabrics and materials. Practice sketching from a new angle or using a new tool. Work on a sewing skill that you haven't mastered yet. The first time you sew in a zipper, it may not look the best. But keep trying. Once you've sewn your tenth, twentieth, or even hundredth zipper, go back and look at your earlier work to see how much you've grown and how far you've come.

The more you invest in your design skills, the more confident you will be. So pack your sketch pad, sewing machine, and confidence, and embrace the world of fashion.

GLOSSARY

accessory: an extra, nonessential object or item that adds to an outfit

apparel: clothing

buyer: a person who purchases fashion to sell on behalf of a retail or online store

collaborate: to work together with others

collection: a group of fashion designs that are released and marketed to the public at the same time, often seasonally

computer-aided design (CAD): software programs that help designers create 2D and 3D digital representations of designs

consumer: a person who shops for and purchases items

custom: an item that is created specially with one person in mind

embellishment: an extra design element or ornamentation that adds to the decorative details of an item

freelance: a type of independent work where you are not affiliated with any specific business or organization

garment: an item of clothing

interpersonal: relating to the social interactions between two or more people

manufacturing: the process of making and producing batches of apparel items

merchandiser: a person who manages retail displays and inventory

multitasking: performing several tasks at the same time

persistence: continuing to strive for a goal without giving up

portfolio: a collection of work and processes of design projects that demonstrates a designer's skills and vision

prototype: an original model or example of a design item

retail: a type of store or online organization that sells goods directly to consumers

scrutinize: to examine something closely

sketching: drawing to share a design

sustainability: relating to the process of creating an item in a way that tries to minimize destruction and damage to the environment

textile: fabric or cloth

trend: a style or greater cultural preference

wholesale: selling large quantities of items for resale, often to retail stores

SOURCE NOTES

32 “In fashion, one . . . day you’re out.”: Heidi Klum, “*Project Runway*:” IMDB, accessed August 22, 2024, https://m.imdb.com/title/tt0437741/quotes/?ref_=tt_trv_qu.

49 “Adaptive fashion opens . . . and brand development.”: Jonathan Kaufman, “Mindset Matters: The Rise Of Adaptive Fashion Awakens More Than Just A Business Opportunity,” *Forbes*, September 23, 2022, https://www.forbes.com/sites/jonathankaufman/2022/09/23/mindset-matters-the-rise-of-adaptive-fashion-awakens-more-than-just-a-business-opportunity/.

51 “Having the right . . . to look at.”: Ellie Violet Bramley, “Is a Lack of Diversity Holding Back the Fashion Industry?” *Guardian*, January 23, 2024, https://www.theguardian.com/fashion/2024/jan/23/fashion-industry-diversity-lack.

SELECTED BIBLIOGRAPHY

Bringé, Alison. "The State of Sustainability in the Fashion Industry (And What It Means for Brands)." *Forbes*. Accessed August 22, 2024. https://www.forbes.com/councils/forbescommunicationscouncil/2023/01/02/the-state-of-sustainability-in-the-fashion-industry-and-what-it-means-for-brands/.

"Fashion Designer." Occupational Outlook Handbook. Accessed August 22, 2024. https://www.bls.gov/ooh/arts-and-design/fashion-designers.htm.

"The Five Stages of the Design Process." Istituto Marangoni Miami. Accessed August 22, 2024. https://www.istitutomarangonimiami.com/blog/the-5-stages-of-the-design-process/.

Ginsberg, Brandon. "Artificial Intelligence in Fashion." *Forbes*. Accessed August 22, 2024. https://www.forbes.com/councils/theyec/2023/02/21/artificial-intelligence-in-fashion/.

"How Will AI Impact the Future of Fashion?" LIM College. Accessed August 22, 2024. https://www.limcollege.edu/blog/how-will-ai-impact-future-fashion.

Reem, Ann Emerson (fashion designer), in discussion with the author, August 26, 2024.

FURTHER INFORMATION

Books

Allaire, Christian. *The Power of Style: How Fashion and Beauty Are Being Used to Reclaim Cultures*. Toronto: Annick Press, 2021.
A fashion and style writer for *Vogue*, the author discusses how fashion connects to larger culture and social issues.

Danneberg, Julie. *The Science of Fashion*. Norwich, VT: Nomad Press, 2021.
The author takes readers on a deep dive into the science behind how clothing is made.

Darke, Tiffanie. *What to Wear and Why: Your Guilt-Free Guide to Sustainable Fashion*. Minneapolis: Broadleaf Books, 2024.
This well-researched book gives helpful information about embracing sustainability in fashion.

Muchnick, Justin Ross. *Teens' Guide to College and Career Planning: Your High School Roadmap to College and Career Success*. Denver: Peterson's, 2022.
This book is a guide to planning for college and how it will help you meet your career goals.

Reeves, Diane Lindsey. *Do You Like Keeping Up with Fashion?* Ann Arbor, MI: Cherry Lake, 2023.
The author presents a brief overview of a variety of career options in the fashion industry.

Websites

The Art Career Project—Careers in Fashion
https://theartcareerproject.com/fashion-careers/
This resource provides a comprehensive overview of careers and schooling options in the fashion industry.

College Navigator
https://nces.ed.gov/collegenavigator/
College Navigator is a helpful search engine to find and research colleges that offer degrees in fashion design.

The Council of Fashion Designers of America, Inc. (CFDA)
https://cfda.com/
The CFDA is a nonprofit membership group driven to strengthen the impact of American fashion design.

Library of Congress—Fashion Industry: A Resource Guide
https://guides.loc.gov/fashion-industry/
The Library of Congress has a comprehensive collection of links and resources to learn more about the fashion industry.

University of California Berkeley Library—Researching Fashion: Popular Fashion Source
https://guides.lib.berkeley.edu/c.php?g=379166&p=2567730
This library site provides an overview of online resources that are helpful in researching and keeping up with trends in fashion.

INDEX

ABOUT THE AUTHOR

Kelley Barth is a former children's librarian who loves connecting with young people over stories and books. When she isn't busy writing, she enjoys reading, hiking, crafting, and going on adventures with her husband and son.

PHOTO ACKNOWLEDGMENTS

Image credits: RossHelen/iStock/Getty Images, p. 5; Thomas Barwick/DigitalVision/Getty Images, p. 7; illustrart/iStock/Getty Images, p. 9; Connect Images/Getty Images, p. 11; Vladimir Vladimirov/E+/Getty Images, p. 13; Hispanolistic/E+/Getty Images, p. 15; Chaosamran_Studio/iStock/Getty Images, p. 16; FOTOGRAFIA INC./E+/Getty Images, p. 18; KatarzynaBialasiewicz/iStock/Getty Images, p. 21; Peathegee Inc/Tetra images/Getty Images, p. 23; Nikada/iStock Unreleased/Getty Images, p. 25; wera Rodsawang/Moment/Getty Images, p. 26; Dimitri's Kambouris/Getty Images for Marc Jacobs/Getty Images, p. 30; Maskot/Getty Images, p. 33; Caia Image/Collection Mix: Subjects/Getty Images, p. 35; SeanShot/E+/Getty Images, p. 38; Dragen Zigic/iStock/Getty Images, p. 40; designer491/iStock/Getty Images, p. 42; SDI Productions/E+/Getty Images, p. 45; gorodenkoff/iStock/Getty Images, p. 47; grinvalds/iStock/Getty Images, p. 48; MoMo Productions/DigitalVision/Getty Images, p. 50; kupicoo/E+/Getty Images, p. 55.

Cover image: Vladimir Vladimirov/E+/Getty Images